**COMING SOON!
T SEES A PYRAMID
T SEES THE COLOSSEUM**

T Sees an Island©

Copyright© 2016 by Tani Lamb

Written by Tani Lamb

Illustrated by Marian Mekhail

All rights reserved. No part of this book may be reproduced or utilized in any form or by any means, electronic or mechanical, including, photocopying, recording, stored in the retrieval system, or transmitted in any form or by any means— electronic, mechanical, scanning, or otherwise, without either the prior written permission from the author, except for the inclusion of brief quotations in a review.

Printed in the United States

10 9 8 7 6 5 4 3 2 1

Thank you to the teachers
Anna Osley Price & LaRoyce Beatty
Thank you to my Aunts
Madaline, Vivian and Sandra
Thank you to the cheerleaders
Makesha, Alisa and Chi
D. Only you can party like a Moko Jumbie!
Thank you, Lauren, for introducing me to an amazing
Illustrator Marian Mekhail
Love you Mom and Paw Paw

Hi there, my name is T. I live in the delightful Commonwealth of Kentucky. It is truly a magical place for children. We have rolling hills filled with bright green grass. The grass is so green, that on sunny summer days, the grass turns blue! You have to look quickly to catch the blue, because when you blink—it turns green again. It's Kentucky's blue magic at work.

We also have super-fast horses in Kentucky. The horses are so fast that we have a special race every year in May. The horse race is called the Kentucky Derby. The horses are so swift. I wonder if they have invisible wings helping them?

Oh, and let's not forget about the Mammoth Cave National Park. The caves tunnel so deep underground that you can make it to the earth's core! The Mammoth Cave system is a giant maze and you can get lost. So, you need a special map to find the earth's center. An adult told me the scientists lost the special map. Because the map is misplaced, we cannot explore the caves right now. Oh well, one day that will make for a great adventure.

Speaking of adventures, I have a grand one to tell you. One day I was in Nina's room. Nina is my big sister. I was looking through her closet and found an enormous brown box. The box was tucked away in a dark corner. I knew the box was for me. How did I know? Because written on the box was, "Nina's box, not T's" in giant bold black letters!

My mom always said, "exploring is an important part of being a child." I then remembered my mother saying, "make sure you return everything to its rightful place." So, I quickly organized the room to cover my tracks. I then focused on the giant brown box. I could not wait to see what surprise was inside.

Immediately, I opened the box. Wow! There seemed to be sparkly gold glitter everywhere. Then I realized that the gold objects were books. The glitter was only on the outer book edges. There were so many books; book after book after book.

Plus—one more thing—a note.

# The note from Nina said,

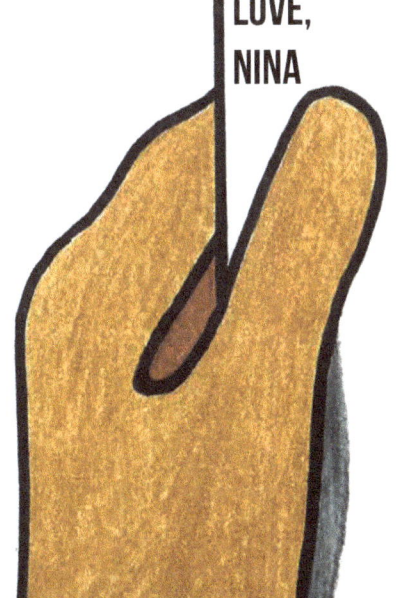
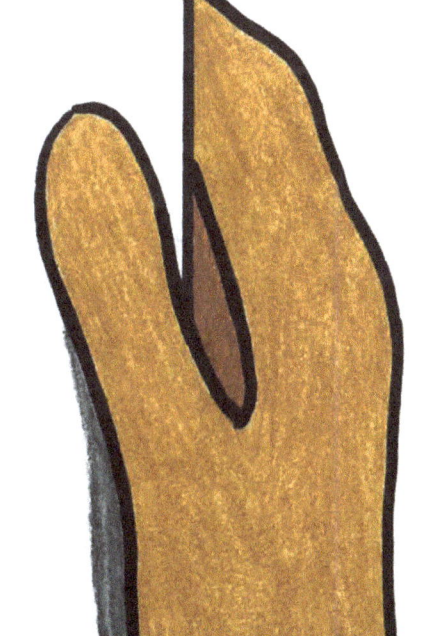

"I KNEW ONE DAY YOU WOULD FIND THIS BOX. YOU ARE ADVENTUROUS AND CURIOUS. YOU ARE ALWAYS SNOOPING (SNOOPING MEANS SEARCHING WITHOUT PERMISSION) IN MY ROOM. I KNOW YOU ARE SNOOPING BECAUSE YOU NEVER RETURN MY THINGS TO WHERE THEY BELONG.

THIS BOX IS FILLED WITH MY MAGICAL ENCYCLOPEDIAS (EN-CY-CLO-PE-DI-A). THE ENCYCLOPEDIAS ARE REFERENCE BOOKS. THEY WERE ONE MY MOST PRIZED CHILDHOOD POSSESSIONS. THEY BROUGHT ME SO MUCH HAPPINESS. THE ENCYCLOPEDIAS ALLOWED ME TO SEE AND DO SO MUCH. I HOPE YOU WILL ENJOY THEM AS MUCH AS I DID."

LOVE,
NINA

I was so excited about my encyclopedias. I had to find out what made them magical. I needed help moving the box. I knew my friend Lee would help. I sent her a text asking her to come over. Lee agreed to help. She arrived quickly. It took a lot of pushing for both of us to move the box of books. We finally got the box into my play room.

In the play room, Lee and I carefully placed the magical encyclopedias on the floor. We soon realized what she meant by reference books. The books ranged from A to Z and were filled with information about every topic. This is what people used before the Internet.

## WOW!

Lee and I tried to decide which book to peek into first. Lee insisted on "L," and I insisted on "T." Suddenly, something wonderful happened. The "U" volume of the encyclopedia spun in a circle and flipped opened!

The pages turned, on their own, to the United States Virgin Islands. The words lit up like a Christmas tree. Our eyes were wide and filled with excitement. Gleefully we screamed, "The United States Virgin Islands!" With one blink, we were standing on a white sand beach.

Lee shouted with excitement, "OMG, T! What just happened?" Palm trees swayed in the breeze. The salty air filled our lungs. Water stretched for as far as our eyes could see. The ocean was flowing in every direction, wave after wave. Yes, we were definitely on an island! There was no Kentucky blue grass in sight.

We were excited, but we needed to confirm our location. There was party music playing off in the distance. We followed the sound. Suddenly, we found a giant! The giant was about twelve feet tall and had wooden legs. His clothing was bright and colorful. He wore a purple top hat tilted on top of his head.

The giant was jumping, singing and dancing. Yet, his purple top hat never slipped. He was having so much fun. We decided to join the party. We finally asked the stilted gentleman, "Are we in the land of giants?" He answered as if he were singing, "No Doll, you are in St. Thomas, and I am a Moko Jumbie. I bring the party. I am the life of the party!"

Oooooooooooh! We were in the United States Virgin Islands! This was so amazing. We sang and danced with the Moko Jumbie and his friends until we could dance no more. Lee then asked, "What other fun things we should do in St. Thomas?" The Moko Jumbie suggested that we visit his home island of St. Croix. We can go snorkeling there. He said there was a special sea plane. The special sea plane had a super engine that would get us there fast. The trip would only take five minutes.

Lee and I shouted, "We get to ride in an airplane too?"

"Yes, but not just an airplane, a sea plane. This special airplane can float and land on water," replied the Moko Jumbie. "The sea plane flies from island to island all of the time."

We skipped to the sea plane. We boarded the plane with much delight. Mr. Moko Jumbie was correct; in five minutes, we were on the beautiful beach in St. Croix.

After a short walk, we arrived at the snorkeling area. It was time to swim in the Caribbean Sea. We had to gear up: fins, check; giant face mask with snorkel, check; sunblock, check; life jackets, check. Lee is a much better swimmer than I am, but that did not matter. We both had to wear life jackets to keep our bodies and our fins on top of the water. We had to avoid harming the coral.

Our guide's name was Mr. Buck. Mr. Buck's job was to keep us safe and to help us identify the animals in the Caribbean Sea. Filled with wonder and excitement the three of us snorkeled off into the colorful coral. It was truly breathtaking!

Lee shouted, "T, what do you see?"

I was captivated by what I saw; the coral was so bright! It was red and looked like fire—fire underwater!

Next, I saw a bright green sea turtle, and he had fins where his little hands should have been. I tried to catch him but he was either pretty fast for a turtle, or I was pretty slow for a human—it was hard to tell.

After losing that race, I focused on all the schools of fish. I saw a blue fish that was thin and flat like a pancake. The blue fish had a bright yellow stripe with a spot of yellow sunshine on his tail. Mr. Buck identified that fish as a banded butterfly fish. As I watched the yellow tail of the banded butterfly fish, I saw a rock watching me. Yes, a rock! The rock's blinking eyes watched me swim. Mr. Buck identified this species as a Rock Fish. Mr. Buck told us that this fish uses camouflage to catch food. Camouflage is the ability to blend in to your surroundings.

Our eyes then focused on a fish with bright neon colors. The neon blue and orange fish was a Queen Angelfish. Her vibrant colors made it appear as though she was glowing underwater.

Swimming along I saw an octopus tucked under a rock. He had one eye showing. "I have my eye on you, too, Mr. Octopus," said T!

Lee joined me and next we saw a group of colorful pincushions. They were not too far away from Mr. one-eyed Octopus. There were different colors like black, white and red. We wanted to touch the pretty pincushions. Some were even small enough to fit into our hands. Mr. Buck swam over and stopped us. He explained that the pincushions were really sea urchins. Some species of sea urchins could deliver a very nasty sting.

Ouch! That was one mistake avoided. My attention was then captured by a racing seahorse. I think the seahorse was trying to win the Kentucky Derby. We swam with the seahorse until the waters got a little deeper. Suddenly, we felt a ripple in the water.

We looked to the left and saw the most striking animal. It was a spotted eagle ray! He was stunning. The eagle ray had polka dots on his back and a smooth white belly underneath. The spotted eagle ray whipped his tail with such grace. Lee and I just paused for a moment to admire him.

Lee suddenly tugged on my arm to tell me a shar…..!

I then heard my mom calling my name. Immediately my thoughts turned to home.

Once my mind returned home, Lee and I were suddenly back in my play room. I asked Lee what she was trying to tell me? Lee said, "I thought that maybe, I might have seen a shark?" We both looked at each other and giggled, maybe!

I closed the encyclopedia before my mother entered my play room. Right away, I noticed something very odd! Lee and I were both 95% dry. We looked almost normal except for two things. Lee's blonde ponytails were dripping a little water and my afro puffs were twice their normal size.

There were also two pairs of souvenirs at our feet. We both had a giant conch shell and a shiny silver and gold hook bracelet. Lee looked at me and said, "T, do you see that?"
"Yes, I see our wonderful gifts, Lee!"

I quickly answered my mother. I did not want her to enter my room and find our new gifts. We returned the "U" volume of the encyclopedia to the box. I hid my souvenirs in my toy chest. Lee gathered her gifts and headed home. We were both so excited. We could not wait for our next adventure, to discover what T will see next!

BERMUDA
FLORIDA
ST. BARTS
ANTIGUA & BARBUDA
ST. MARTIN
U.S. VIRGIN ISLANDS
ST. THOMAS
ST. CROIX
ST. JOHN
ST. KITTS & NEVIS
MONSERRAT
BAHAMAS
DOMINICA
MARTINIQUE
ST. LUCIA
TURKS AND CAICOS
ST. VINCENT AND THE GRENADINES
HAITI
DOMINICAN REPUBLIC
GRENADA
PUERTO RICO
JAMAICA
NICARAGUA
ARUBA
CURACAO
BARBADOS
BONAIRE
PANAMA
VENEZUELA
COLOMBIA
M&M 2017

**TANI LAMB**
WORLD TRAVELER

Tani Lamb's ardent love for adventure and penchant for history began as a child. Tani attended church every Sunday. Her paternal grandfather was the pastor and her grandmother taught bible lessons. Frequent interstate church revivals exposed Tani to numerous Midwestern and Southern towns and aroused her curiosity about faraway lands. An adventurous young child matured into a 'world traveler' where she saw, firsthand, the countries she had only read about in books. Her vicarious travels soon became real-life expeditions into foreign countries. Tani has visited over 30 states in the United States, six of the seven continents and 35 countries.

The colorful pictures of other ethnic groups, and stories about diverse cultures, were once mere pages in a book. Now, Tani's curiosity has been replaced with vivid memories of distant lands, those she has seen with her own eyes. She believes that every person, old and young, should let their imagination design a travel plan to "see the world." Tani firmly believes that traveling enables us to experience the kindness, hospitality, cultures and values of our neighbors all over the world. This belief motivated Tani to write the "T Sees!" series of children's books. Her first book, "T sees an Island" opens the lid on Tani's box of enchanted travels.

www.ingramcontent.com/pod-product-compliance
Lightning Source LLC
Chambersburg PA
CBHW080520020526
44113CB00055B/2538